LANG LANG PIANO ACADEMY

THE LANG LANG PIANO METHOD

Have fun becoming a superhero pianist with Lang Lang!

This book belongs to:

_____

My teacher's name is:

_____

FABER *ff* MUSIC

CONTENTS

© 2016 by Faber Music Ltd and Lang Lang
All rights administered by Faber Music Ltd
This edition first published in 2016
Bloomsbury House 74-77 Great Russell Street London WC1B 3DA
Music processed by Musicset2000
Illustrations by Lauren Appleby
Page design by Susan Clarke
Audio demonstrations by Christopher Hussey
Concert pieces performed by Lang Lang at the Royal College of Music
Printed in England by Caligraving Ltd
All rights reserved.

Lang Lang: worldwide management – Jean-Jacques Cesbron
CAMI Music, New York (www.camimusic.com)
Lang Lang: UK/Ireland management – Steve Abbott,
Rainbow City Broadcasting Ltd (www.rainbowcity.co)

ISBN10: 0-571-53913-0
EAN13: 978-0-571-53913-0

LANG LANG

INTERNATIONAL
MUSIC FOUNDATION

Hi, I'm Lang Lang! Welcome to the wonderful world of the piano. You're on your way to becoming a superhero pianist like me now – let's carry on!

You can hear all the pieces on the online audio* and you can hear me play the concert piece in each section. The audio gives two bars of count-in clicks for each piece.

Keep playing the piano every day and always perform as beautifully as you can.

* Scan the QR code or go to:
www.fabermusic.com/LangLangPianoMethodDownloads

WELCOME BACK!

Hooray – welcome back! Look out for any flat and natural signs. Can you remember what they mean?

CONCERT PIECE

Track 1 THEME AND VARIATIONS

after Wolfgang Amadeus Mozart

Theme

With singing tone

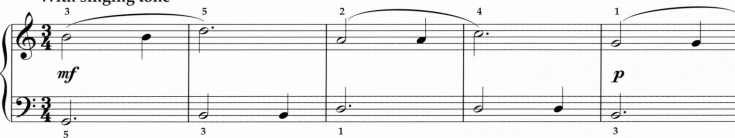

Variation 1

Solemn and expressive

16

cresc.

Variation 2

Lively and cheerful

21

f

mp

REMINDER
rit. = slow down.

26

cresc.

f

rit.

5

A SUPERHERO SCALE

You've learnt how to put your thumb under so now you're ready to play a whole scale.

Track ② **C MAJOR SCALE WARM-UP**

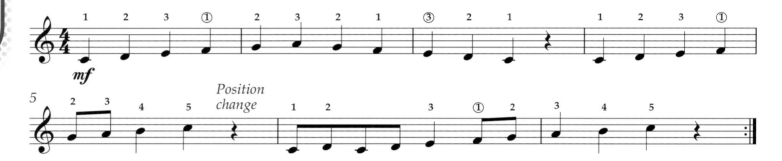

Track ③ **ON A SWING**

TIP
Learn the right hand by itself first.

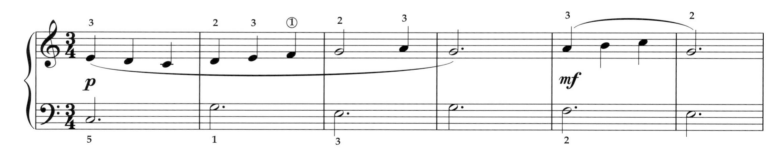

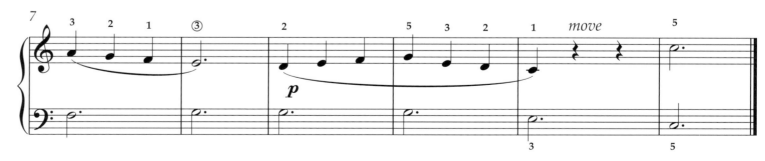

Reminder: D.C. al Fine = go back to the beginning and play again as far as 'Fine'.

New notes
C B

I love scales – I play them every day!

Track ④

C MAJOR SCALE WARM-UP

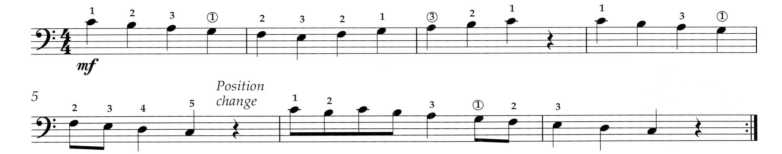

mf

5 | Position change

Track ⑤

TOY SOLDIER MARCH

TIP
Learn the left hand first.

Fine

mf

move

5

1. *2.* **D.C. al Fine**

p

7

The finger swaps are boxed. Can you circle any big leaps?

These signs are also known as **hairpins**.
   = **crescendo** = getting louder
   = **decrescendo** = getting quieter (**diminuendo**)

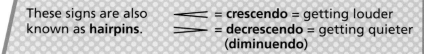

Track 6 — FINGER SWAPS

Track 7 — BIG LEAPS

Track 8 — CAN-CAN

Jacques Offenbach

With steady movement

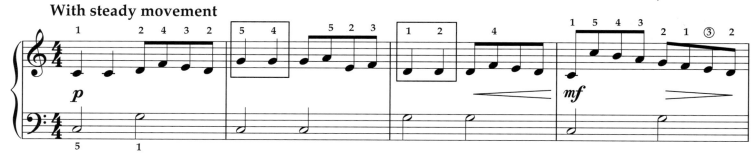

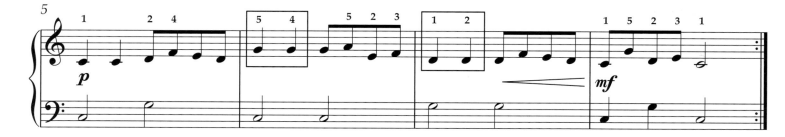

ON MY TRAVELS

Minor scales sound serious!

Track
⑩ **A MINOR SCALE WARM-UP**

This is a natural minor scale.

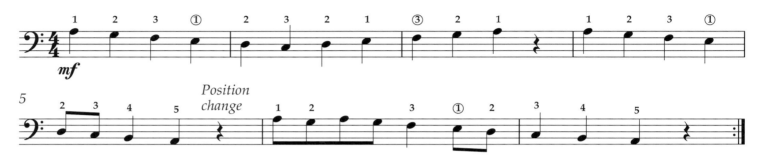

Track
⑪ **OLD RUSSIAN CASTLE BY THE RIVER**

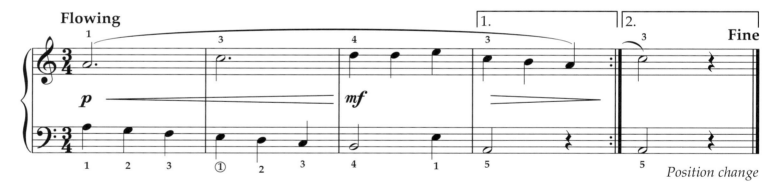

Position change

rit.   **D.C. al Fine with repeat**

Position change   *Position change*

A MINOR SCALE WARM-UP

A RUSSIAN TALE

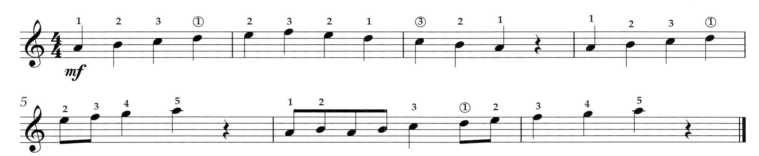

Expressively

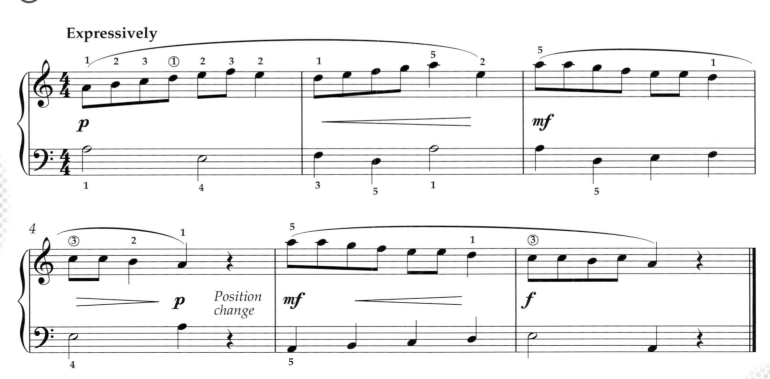

Position change

11

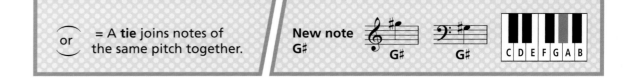

or = A **tie** joins notes of the same pitch together.

New note G♯

Here is your first harmonic minor scale. It has an exotic sound!

Track (14) **A HARMONIC MINOR WARM-UPS**

Track (15) **SNAKE CHARMER**   Can you spot the ties and one position change in the left hand?

With mystery

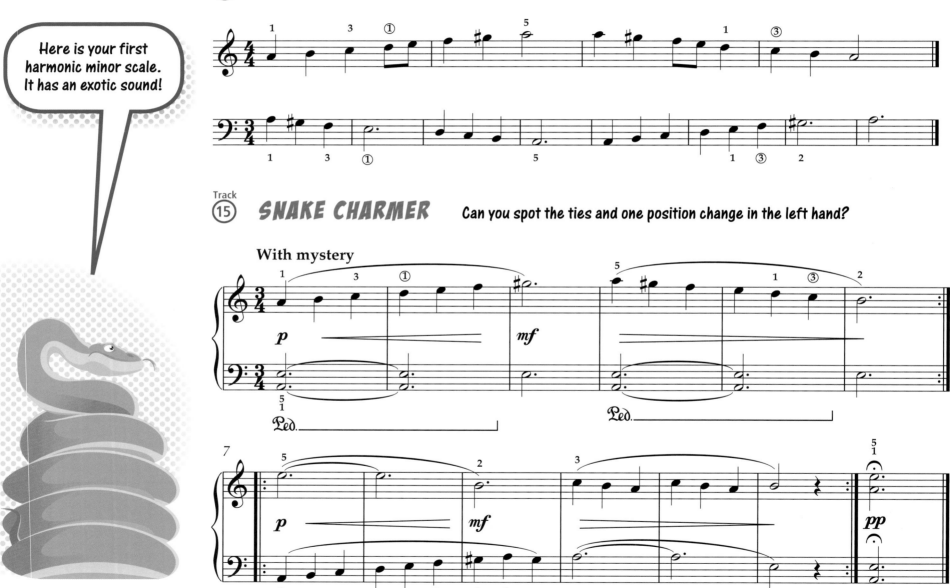

This piece contains chords that are 5ths and 6ths. See page 18 for more about intervals.

PROCESSION OF THE ELEPHANTS

Can you find any changes of hand position yourself?

CONCERT PIECE

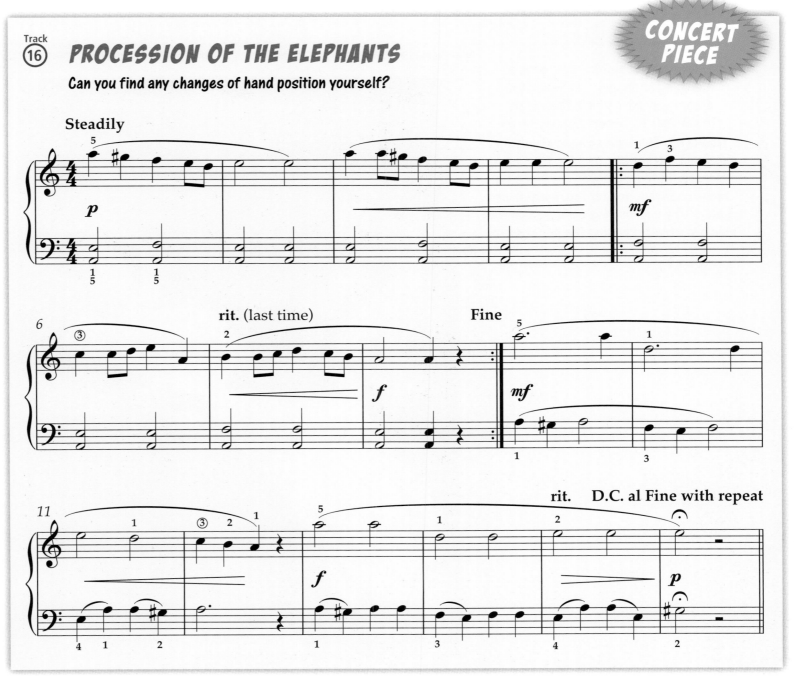

TAKE A BREAK

This beautiful picture of a woman sleeping is the perfect image to accompany me playing *Träumerei* (Dreaming) by Robert Schumann on track ⑰. The tune sweeps slowly up and down, rather like dreams floating up to space. In the middle of the piece the mood changes: does it feel happier or sadder? Try improvising some dream-like music yourself, keeping the pedal down.

Mary Evans / Retrograph Collection

LANG LANG'S THEORY NOTEBOOK

Fill in the clouds:

Name the note:

_____

mf means:

_____

_____

How many beats?

_____

D.C. al Fine means:

_____

_____

Name the note:

_____

Rit. means:

_____

_____

A tempo means:

_____

_____

What is this?

_____

_____

Name the rest:

_____

Name the note:

_____

How many beats?

_____

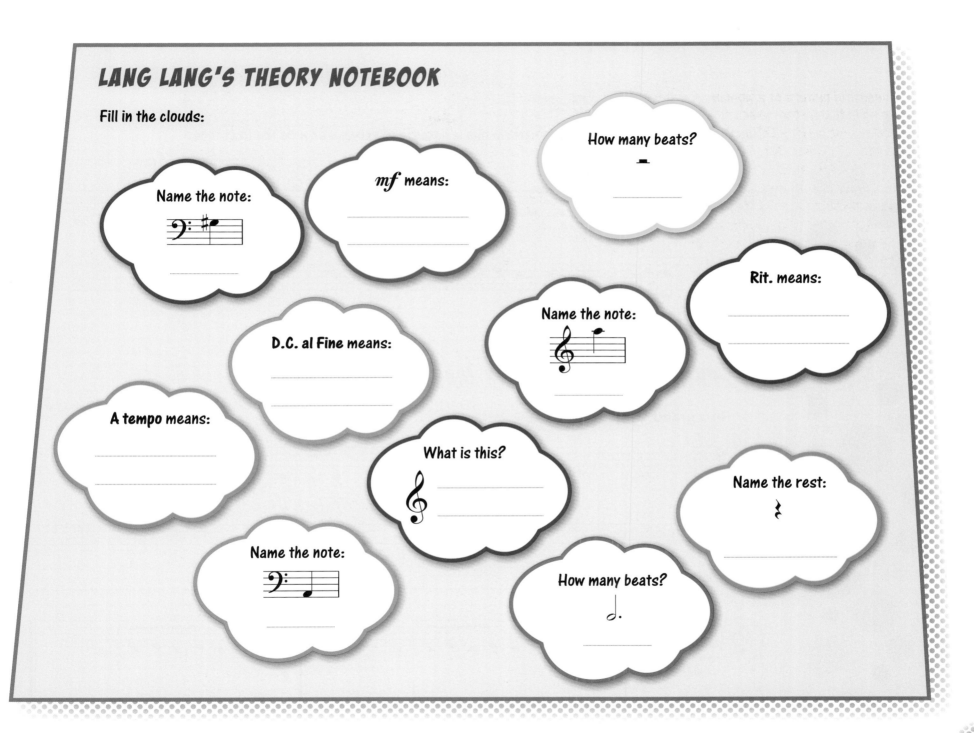

DOTTED SUPERHEROES

A dot after a note adds half as much again to its value:

Track
(18) **DOTTED WARM-UP**

Clap the left-hand rhythm first. The new rhythm is boxed, and shown with a tie the first time.

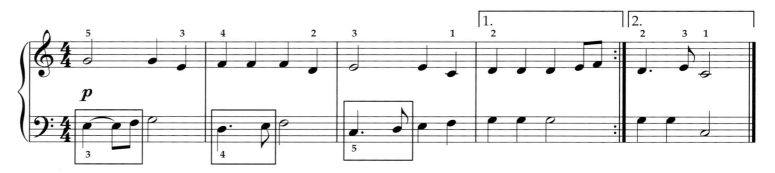

Track
(19) **PRINCE OF DENMARK'S MARCH**

Jeremiah Clarke

In a grand style

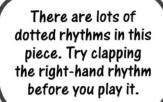

There are lots of dotted rhythms in this piece. Try clapping the right-hand rhythm before you play it.

Track
20 **NEW WORLD SYMPHONY THEME**

Antonín Dvořák

Slow and expressive

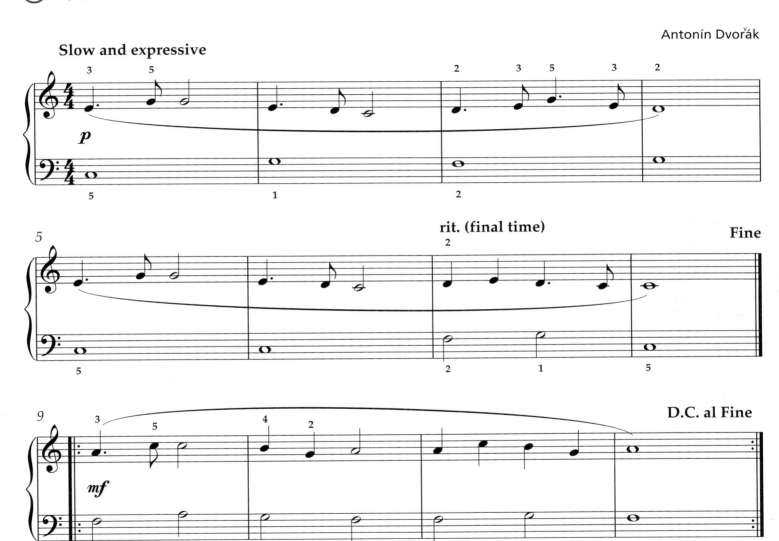

17

> You will need to extend your hand to play the larger intervals.

Track 21 **INTERVAL WARM-UP**

> The distance between two notes is called the **interval**. You can work out an interval by counting up (or down) all the notes.

You will have to extend your hand to play this.

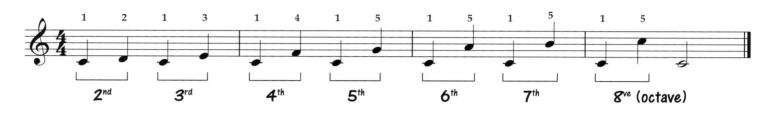

Track 22 **INTERVAL WARM-DOWN**

Can you work out these intervals yourself?

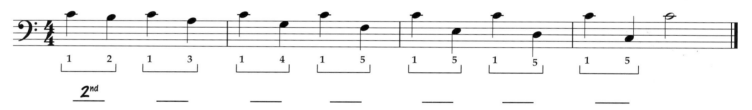

Track 23 **CHORDS ON PARADE**

> Chords are also made up of intervals. Can you work out the interval of each chord?

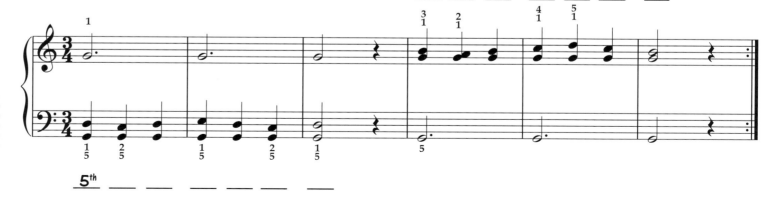

18

New note E♭

Can you work out the intervals of the left-hand chords? You'll have to extend your hand and move hand position in this piece.

Track 24

GRAND PIANO BOOGIE

CONCERT PIECE

With a steady groove

19

MORE SUPERHERO SCALES

A **key signature** appears at the start of each line of music. It shows which sharps or flats should be played through the whole piece. An F sharp shows that you are in G major.

Track
(25) **G MAJOR SCALE WARM-UPS**

Circle any black notes before you play.

Here are some more scales for you to learn. Look out for any black notes.

Track
(26) **THE GIRAFFE** The key signature shows you need to play F sharps.

20

⁷ = eighth-note (quaver) rest.

The short measure (bar) at the start of this piece is called an **upbeat**. The final one is shortened by the value of the upbeat.

New note D♯

D♯

F G A B C D E

Track (27)

Wolfgang Amadeus Mozart

Mozart's joke was to have a surprise at the end!

With fun

21

Track 28

A CONTRARY-MOTION SCALE

CHALLENGE
Can you add the fingering yourself?

Try this hands separately first.

Watch out! You will have to extend your hands to play this broken-chord study.

Track 29

STRETCHING STUDY

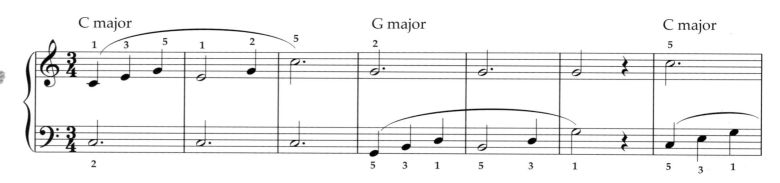

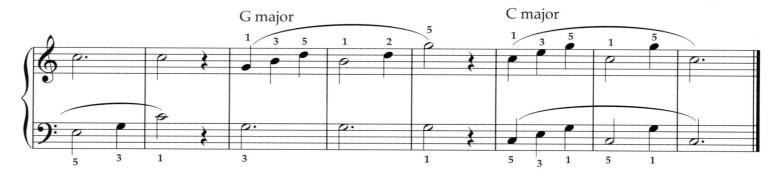

An **arpeggio** is made up of the 1st, 3rd, 5th and 8th notes of a scale.

Can you see any arpeggios in *Cartwheel calypso*?

Track ③⓪ **CARTWHEEL CALYPSO**

Cheerfully

TAKE A BREAK

LANG LANG'S THEORY NOTEBOOK

Name, add fingering and any sharps needed to these scales, then play them:

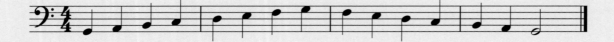

Write these tied notes out as a single notes:

Name these notes and rests:

....

LANG LANG'S THEORY NOTEBOOK

Name the intervals:

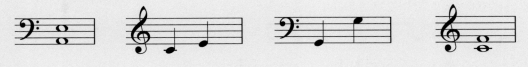

_____   _____   _____   _____

Add barlines:

Add time signatures:

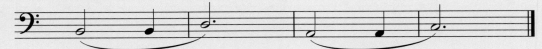

Complete your own tune, based on the scale of C major, then play it!

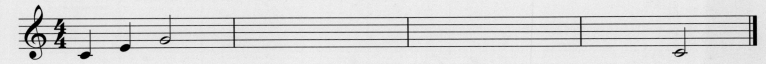

A NEW TIME SIGNATURE

$\frac{3}{8}$ = count 3 eighth-note (quaver) beats in a measure (bar).

This is interesting – we're counting in ♪ not ♩ now. It makes the music feel different!

Clap and count this $\frac{3}{8}$ rhythm:

Track 31

Track 32 **MORNING STUDY**   Remember to count 3 x ♪ in a measure (bar).

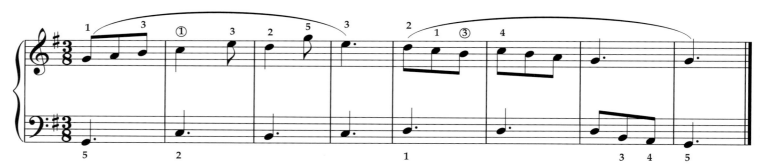

Track 33 **EVENING STUDY**   Try the left hand on its own first.

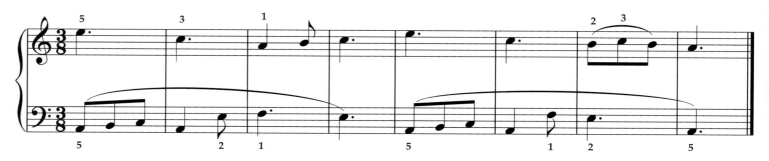

Track
34 **COWBOY SONG**

Reminder
𝄾 = eighth-note (quaver) rest.

New note D

BARCAROLLE

CONCERT PIECE

Jacques Offenbach

Gently swaying

TIP
Work on right-hand measures 12–15 before trying hands together.

gradually slowing down

SCALE REVIEW

Here's your scale review.

Try to play at least one scale a day.

C MAJOR

G MAJOR

A HARMONIC MINOR

Play G natural for A natural minor and G♯ for A harmonic minor.

29

LET'S CELEBRATE!

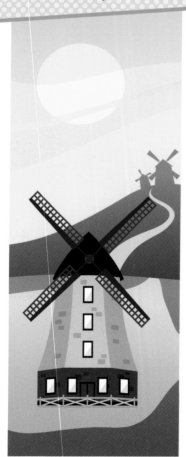

D.C. al Coda = go back to the beginning and play until you reach ⊕, then go straight to Coda.

Sim. = **simile** = continue in a similar way.

Track ㊱ *THE WINDMILL*

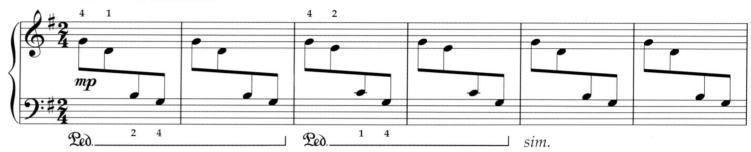

Smooth and balanced

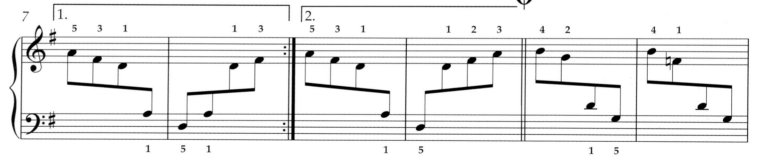

last time to Coda ⊕

D.C. al Coda (with repeat) ⊕ CODA

30

CELEBRATION RAG

CONCERT PIECE

Cheerful and rhythmic

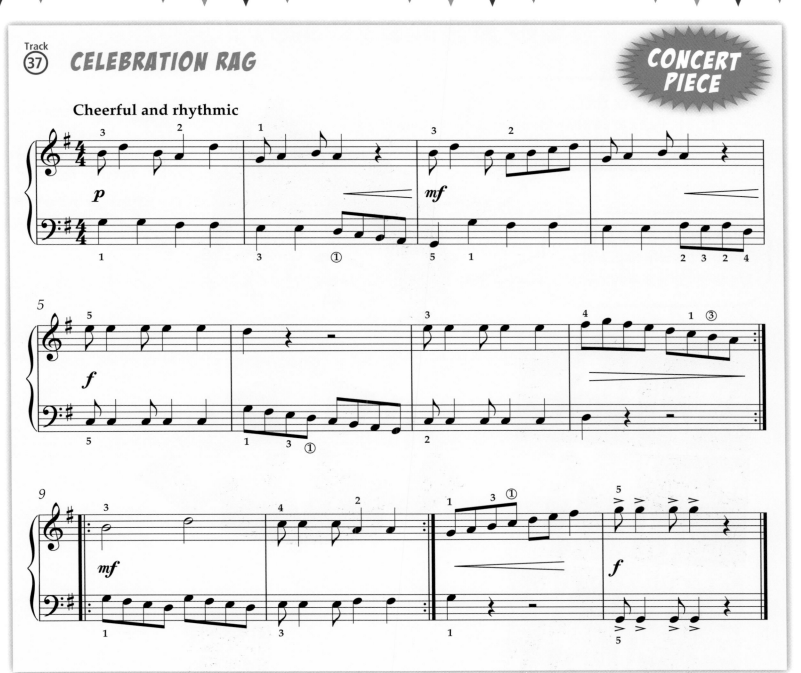

CONGRATULATIONS!

You've finished Level 3 and are ready to move up to Level 4!

Remember, it's great to do lots of listening. Here are some of my albums …

Download a certificate for your teacher to sign.*

GOOD WORK!

YOU'RE READY TO MOVE UP TO LEVEL 4

SIGNED _____
(TEACHER)

* Scan the QR code or go to:
www.fabermusic.com/LangLangPianoMethodDownloads